Where do you live?

On the edge of a housing estate in south Wales. Roads often act as unofficial boundaries of communities.

- **Can you suggest some reasons why this might be?**

They call this part 'Hanky Park'.

It is that district opposite the parish church of Pendleton, one of the many industrial townships comprising the Two Cities. In the early nineteenth century Hanky Park was part of the grounds of a wealthy lady's mansion; (. . .) The district takes its name from a sloping street, Hankinson Street, whose pavements, much worn and very narrow, have been polished by the traffic of boots and clogs for many generations. On either side of this there are other streets, mazes, jungles of tiny houses cramped and huddled together (. . .) public houses by the score (. . .) pawnshops by the dozen (. . .) churches, chapels and unpretentious mission halls. . .

From Love on the Dole, by Walter Greenwood, Penguin

The passage above describes a poor part of Salford in Lancashire in the 1930s. The book describes life in the area — the relationships between the people living there and what happens to them all.

- If you were going to write a book about your area, how would you describe it? Try writing an introduction like the one above, explaining where the area you are writing about is and what you think is its character.

The first thing you are going to have to decide on is exactly what 'your area' is. Suppose it is the area around the school, or near your home. What would you say are its boundaries?

Is there a main road or railway, the other side of which you would say is not 'your area'?

- Draw a map of the area that covers your community.

Now carry out a survey, using note books or tape recorders. Find out:

Does everyone agree with your ideas of where the boundaries are?

Do people feel they belong there? How long have most lived there?

Do they like the place? Are the neighbours friendly? Do many people have relatives nearby?

What sort of housing is there? Is it a council estate, or privately rented? Do most people own their own homes?

Are the houses old or new? Is the area rich or poor?

Are most people working class or middle class? What sorts of jobs do they do?

Are the shops, pubs, cinemas and so on handy?

Your findings should give you a clear picture of the character of the community you have been studying as well as the facts about the place. How do they compare with those of others in your class?

A second look

Now you've drawn up a picture of the area in which you live, take another look at it. Is it a good, happy friendly place to live? Are there plenty of things to do? Do the people help one another?

The information you have so far might give a clue about some of the needs of the people in your area, and whether or not the place is the sort of community in which people get help and support from their neighbours. Taking your survey a little further, work out what sorts of things could be done to improve life for people in your community.

● If your area is not the sort of place that could really be called 'a community', if it is the sort of place where few people feel they belong, know their neighbours or care about the area, suggest some ways of bringing people together to form a community — if the money and facilities were available.

What can they do?

Mary is twenty-four. She has been married for three years and has a two-year-old son and a baby daughter. Her husband works long hours in order to save money to buy a house, so she doesn't get much chance to talk to him. Sometimes she feels rather angry about this. The family live on the top floor flat in a big house. They have no garden.

Before she had the children, Mary was a secretary. She enjoyed her job and liked the company it gave her. Now she feels lonely, trapped and bored.

Bill is seventy-six and not in the best of health. His wife, who was older than him, died last year. While she was alive, Bill spent a lot of his time looking after her. Now he is at a bit of a loose end. Occasionally he takes a walk to the pub but, as he has to live on his pension, he can't afford to spend much money there. His house, which he owns, is in a bad state of repair and he cannot afford to have it put right.

Fred is in his early thirties. His wife left him four years ago with two young daughters, now aged eight and six. Looking after the children has made things difficult for Fred, but he has managed to stay in work. But he is often faced with the problem of what to do with the children after school, in the holidays, and when they are ill. Sometimes a neighbour can help, sometimes his mother comes to stay, but he can't rely on either.

● There are all sorts of organizations that might be able to help these people. Advice and practical aid is available from the local authority and from voluntary bodies. (See below.) List the problems these people have or might have and, from reference books and other resources, find out how much help they might get.

National Marriage Guidance Council
Social worker, social services
Mother and toddler groups
Playgroups
Task Force
Age Concern
National Council for One-parent Families
Gingerbread
Housing Action Areas
The local church
Women's Royal Voluntary Service (WRVS)
Women's groups

● Do you think it is the duty of the local authority to provide for everyone's needs, or is there an advantage in depending on voluntary bodies? Ask people with experience of both what they think, and report on the answers you get.

Two community workers take an old person to a Christmas party for local pensioners. For those without families to befriend them, this sort of activity can be invaluable.

The Community Centre, Penrhys south Wales. Where the traditions of a long-established community do not exist, a place where people can meet may have to be deliberately planned.
A community centre may offer leisure facilities, advice centres, nurseries, clubs and so on.

Case study: Centreprise, a community centre

Centreprise is a community based bookshop in Hackney, east London. The area it serves is typical of many poorer inner city areas—the population is declining, housing is bad.

It was decided to base the project on a bookshop for a number of reasons (. . .) no other bookshop existed in the area (. . .) to open a bookshop in a working class borough like Hackney was to make an important statement about the need to resist the way in which cultural choices were being eroded by commercial priorities.
From Centreprise Annual Report, 1978

Centreprise opened in 1971, funded by a number of bodies including some charitable foundations and the Inner London Education Authority. It is a bookshop with an adjoining coffee bar which can also be used for poetry reading and film shows. The walls often show exhibitions of local people's work just as the bookshop stocks publications by local people. It also carries childrens books, publications for minority interests and Open University text books.

Both the bookshop and the coffee bar are well supported by local people.

In addition to the shops, there are rooms used by organizations such as the local squatters campaign, the claimants union and so on. Centreprise now also runs an advice centre and a publishing project for local writers. Other organizations based at Centreprise include the Hackney Under-Fives Committee (a pressure group for better provisions for pre-school children), a nursery, the Hackney Play Association (concerned with all aspects of children's play), Hackney Worker's Educational Association and a girl's project.

Catering for special needs

Centreprise is a community project especially tailored to suit the needs of its area. What would you say are the special needs of your area?

● Find out:

Is there a community centre in your area? Who funds it? Who runs it?
Is there a law centre?
A citizens advice bureau?
Any specialist centre such as one for people with drug or drink problems?

Do you think there is a need for all or any of these organizations? Do you think they should be given more encouragement and money?

Meeting places

Friendly gatherings

'For entertainment we had two cinemas (. . .) All within reasonable distance. There was nothing here on the estate (. . .) We used to have several 'get togethers' in the flat on a Saturday night. You'd get some beer in and you'd make life what it was.'

From A Street Door of Our Own, published by the Honor Oak Estate Neighbourhood Association. Time: the 1930s.

'Fordlow might boast its church, its school, its annual concert (. . .) but the hamlet (Lark Rise) did not envy these amenities for it had its own social centre, warmer more human and altogether preferable in the taproom of the "Wagon and Horses".

There the adult male population gathered every evening to sip its half pints (. . .)

It was an innocent enough gathering. None of them got drunk; they had not money enough (. . .) Yet the parson preached (against it) (. . .) going so far (. . .) on one occasion as to call it a "den of iniquity".'

From Lark Rise to Candleford by Flora Thompson. Penguin. Time: the late 1800s.

'. . . The Welfare Hall (. . .) To the youth of Ashton (. . .) especially between seventeen and twenty years old, it is an institution of vital importance.

Here each Saturday night there is a dance attended by 400-500 young people (. . .) It is at these dances that the male and female social worlds of Ashton intersect for long enough to make courtship and marriage possible. . .

There are six working men's clubs in Ashton (. . .)

There are also seven pubs which fulfil broadly similar functions. Club members are nearly all men (. . .)

The main activity is simply talking over beer. Conversation is free and easy (. . .) The two main topics are work, the incidents of the day and sport . . .'

From Communities in Britain by Ronald Frankenberg, Penguin (information from Coal is Our Life by N. Dennis, F. M. Henriques and C. Slaughter, Eyre and Spottiswoode). Time: the 1950s.

Main picture and inset: shared interests and hobbies provide an opportunity to meet and make friends.

A chance to talk

A community is more than a row of houses. It is a place where people feel they belong, where they know and care about one another.

None of this is likely to be true of a place unless the people there have the chance to meet one another to relax together and talk.

Most societies have meeting places. They may serve a particular part of the community — the young, the old, the men and so on. In many parts of Europe, particularly the south, the most common sort of meeting place is the café. It can be indoors, sometimes quite smart, or it can be in the open air, like the one in the picture.

In Britain the most widely used meeting places are public houses or 'pubs'. These are not popular with everyone and, as you can see from the piece from *Lark Rise to Candleford,* have been roundly condemned in the past.

- Look carefully at the passages opposite. They all describe places where people met together at some time in the past. Try to think of their equivalents today. (They might not be all that different.)
- Make a chart to show where the people you know (of various ages) spend their leisure time.
- Write a play with a pub, a youth club or any other popular meeting place as a setting. What sort of people will meet there and what will they have to say to one another?
- Make a list of all the clubs, pubs, sports centres and similar places in your area. Which are most popular with which age groups? Why?

Are there noticable differences among different age groups? Between the sexes? Do people travel far to meet one another or do they do so locally? Do any one group — say, the younger ones — tend to travel more than (say) the older ones? Is this connected with the people they want to meet, the particular place they want to meet in (say, a sports centre) or for what other reason?

More meeting places. Top: a 'Darby and Joan' club for the elderly. Above: in southern Europe and many other parts of the world the most popular meeting place is the café. Many, like this Greek one, are mainly used by men. Left: even a launderette can be a meeting place, as can other shared facilities.

Country life

Life in the countryside has changed dramatically over the last 100 years. Modern farming is big business, and even the look of the countryside has changed in many places to accommodate changes in farming methods. Socially, too, the countryside has changed. The writer Laurie Lee in his book *Cider with Rosie,* describes village life in the 1920s, and how an era came to an end:

'The year revolved around the village, the festivals around the year, the church around the festivals, the Squire round the church and the village round the Squire. The Squire was our centre, a crumbling moot tree; and few indeed of our local celebrations could take place without his shade.'

'The death of the Squire was not the end of the church, though they drew to their end together. He died, and the Big House was sold by auction and became a Home for Invalids. The lake silted up, the swans flew away, and the great pike choked in the reeds. With the Squire's hand removed we fell apart — though we were about to do so anyway. His servants dispersed and went into the factories. His nephew broke up the estate.'

From Cider with Rosie by Laurie Lee, Penguin

- Study the passages above and find out from this and other books about the way in which class divisions played an important part in country life in the past (do you think they still do?) Compare the village community described here with what you know of city communities, which were more likely to be made up of one class of people.
- Find out all you can about living in the country today. If you live in the country, you may be able to ask older people in your neighbourhood to tell you what they remember. Are farms larger or smaller? Do they employ more or fewer people than say, 50 years ago? What other changes have happened (particularly in mechanization) since then?
- The traditions of village life were important to Laurie Lee. Try to find out about any traditional customs still kept in country places. If there are any that are still kept in your area, trace their origins and say whether you think it is still worth keeping them.

A country home

Lots of people dream of owning a cottage in the country.

Although only two per cent of people in Britain own second homes (compared with 10 per cent in France and 20 per cent in Sweden), there are often large numbers together and there can be problems for the surrounding community.

1. Second home owners are usually richer than local people. If an area is popular for second homes, then house prices rise out of the reach of local people. In Gwynedd, in Wales, 35 per cent of all marketable properties are second homes, yet local incomes are only 60 per cent of the national average. With homes so hard to find, council waiting lists are long — there are 4,269 names of the list in Gwynedd, yet 7,500 houses there are second homes.
2. Local people become resentful. In Wales in 1979 and 1980 there were deliberately-started fires in holiday homes.
3. Villages die out of season. The sparse permanent population will have to travel miles to reach medical services and schools. Community life suffers — the village of Rhyd, in North Wales for example is almost deserted in winter.
4. The character of the place is lost. Welsh Nationalist MP Dafydd Wigley has said: 'Large areas of West and North Wales are in danger of being no more Celtic in character than the Lake District or Cornwall today.'

- Write a play about a family staying for the first time in their holiday home. Most neighbours are quite friendly, but a few object. The scene is the village pub, the older members of the new family are having their first drink with the locals.
- Write a poem about a deserted village in winter.

In the past in the country, (far more than in the town) the church was of great importance to local people. The vicar was one of the most influential people in the community, friendly with, if not related to, the Squire. Both expected church attendance from villagers and farm workers.

Farm workers

In a farming community, the relationship between a worker and his or her employer is much closer than between their city equivalents.

Farm workers — who now, of course, make up a much smaller percentage of country-dwellers than in the past — often work alongside their boss. They may have been with him for years and know his family well. They work in very small numbers and often live in property he owns.

This puts the farmer in a very powerful position and can make life hard for both farmer and worker if they do not get along very well.

Until 1977, when the Agricultural Rent Act came into force, a farm worker who lost his job would probably also lose his home. Now a farmer cannot get a farm cottage back unless he can prove to an independent panel that he needs the house — and then the farm worker must be offered suitable alternative council housing.

● What sort of difference do you think this law might make to the relationship between a farmer and his workers?

Agricultural wages are low — in 1979 the minimum was £58 a week, though at some times of the year there is a lot of overtime. Only about 50 per cent of agricultural workers are unionised.

● Suggest some reasons why farm workers, though their pay is not high and their hours are long, are not as widely unionised as some other groups of workers.

Town and country

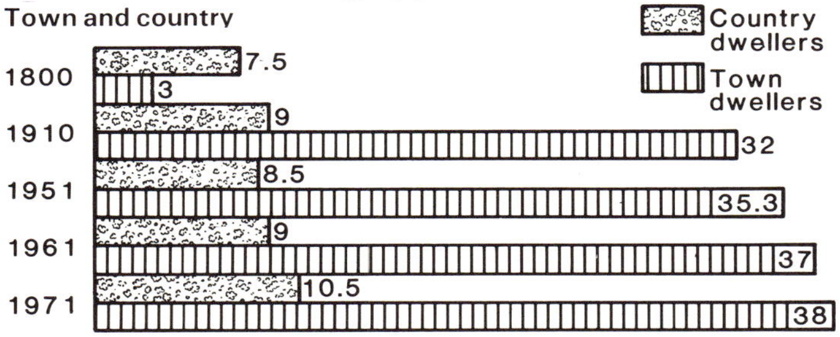

Above: times change — but many people still live in houses designed for another age. This one is in the Orkneys. Below left: the proportion of people living in the country today is only a fraction of what it was. The reason (below, right) is partly because of changing farming methods, requiring fewer people.

Role play

● The scene is a large farm. There are three workers, two older men who live in tied cottages and a younger man who lives with his parents. The older men have children, are married and have children.

Pay is little above the national minimum and, although the men are quite friendly with the farmer, they have a number of grievances. The younger man thinks the best way to solve the problem is for them all to join the union. The two older ones have doubts. Act out the discussions on the matter among the workers, and the discussions that follow with the farmer.

Left: poverty in London's East End, 1912

Looking back

'Haven't you ever wondered what life was like for "ordinary" people centuries ago? Not only people in general but perhaps your ancestors (. . .) Haven't you ever wished that you could get a glimpse into the lives of your past relatives. . .'
From A Licence to Live by Ron Barnes, Centreprise Trust Limited

This part of the book is about trying to get a glimpse into the past in a city community.

The poverty shown in the picture opposite may seem rather depressing and it's certainly true that not everyone a hundred or so years ago was poor. But a very low standard of living — much lower than that we expect today — was commonplace for working class people. In 1889, a wealthy merchant named Charles Booth did research in London that proved that *one in three people* were poor ('living under a struggle to obtain the necessaries of life').

Ten years later, Seebohm Rowntree found about the same degree of poverty in York, and went on to point out that many more people had had experience of poverty at some time in their lives — while they were children, when they had young children, while they were bearing children and in old age.

- From reference books, find out about the work of Seebohm Rowntree. Compare his findings about points in their lives when people were at their poorest with the situation today, and see if they are similar.

In the early years of this century, a young American writer named Jack London disguised himself as a sailor and went to live in London's East End. What he saw shocked him. He describes how thousands of families lived: 'A brief examination of (. . .) as dwelling (. . .) Here the family arises in the morning, dresses and makes its toilet, father mother, sons and daughters, and in the same room, shoulder to shoulder (for the room is small), the wife and mother cooks the breakfast (. . .) The father goes to work, the elder children go to school and the mother remains with her (. . .) youngsters (. . .) Here she washes the clothes, filling the pent space with soap suds and the smell of dirty clothes (. . .)

Here, in the evening, amid the manifold smells of the day (. . .) as many as possible pile into one bed (. . .)'

'Fifty-five per cent of East End children die before they are five years old, the body is laid out in the same room (. . .)'
From The People of The Abyss by Jack London, The Journeyman Press

● Using your local libraries, records offices, back numbers of local papers, parish records and the memories of older people in your neighbourhood, find out what life was like there in the past. What have been the main changes in the last 100 years?

Some of the things you might compare are: the sizes of families, how much people earned, how much they had to spend on basic necessities, what these necessities were, what sort of social services (if any) there were, who provided these, whether people went to church or not, what sorts of homes people lived in, how crowded these were, what sort of education people had, what sorts of jobs they had and how hard they worked. Did they ever get a holiday or a chance to travel?

● Compare the lives of people in the past in your neighbourhood with the description Jack London gave of East End life. Were things better or worse?

● If you had lived in your neighbourhood 100 years ago and were able to look at it today, would you recognize the place? Imagine that this has happened to you and describe your feelings as you walk around the streets.

● Now imagine you are very old, living at some time in the future. Write about your memories of your community.

● Poverty can be described in two ways. It can simply mean not having enough to live on, as Rowntree described it, or it can mean not having enough money to live as society thinks is desirable. Make a list of the things you think are essential in order to live comfortably. Would your parents have made the same list when they were young? Your grandparents? Great grandparents? Why are the lists different?

Memories

● Look at the memories printed below. They describe life in a pre-war housing estate. Compare the things people had to say about your own neighbourhood today. Do you think that people were friendlier is the past? Why?

'As kids we used to nick potatoes and take them down to where the nursery is and roast them. They had a big fire down there. Do you remember rolling paper and smoking?'

'Policemen are different today. If you got up to a piece of mischief they'd say ''I know you'' and he'd thump you and that's the end of it. They can't do that today.'

'Everybody used to leave their doors open and you used to come in and hide behind the door. Nobody used to shout ''Get out of here'' like they do today.'
From A Street Door of Our Own

Top: better-off Victorians, like these were inclined to think that the poor could solve their problems by thrift and hard work. Their sympathies were likely to be reserved for the 'deserving' poor.

Right: war's effect on city life — London children in 1940, evacuated to Truro, Cornwall. 'I remember having a label put on me and going to Mile End Underground,' writes a London woman. 'It was my first experience of going away. (She was four). (...) I didn't even know what my mum and dad looked like when I came home after the war.' *(From Where's your horns? Spitalfields Books)*

● What memories, if any, do your parents have of community life in World War II?

RAILWAY
FLATS
STATION
CHURCH
FIREMEN AT WORK
DUSTMEN AT WORK
PUBLIC GARDENS
HEALTH CENTRE
CORNER SHOP
HIGH STREET
POST OFFICE
BUS SERVICE
SUPERMARKET
LIBRARY
COMMUNITY CENTRE
HOSPITAL AND AMBULANCE
COUNCIL HOUSES
PLAYGROUND
PRIMARY SCHOOL

Who does what?

Look at the picture on the opposite page. It shows a part of a town, the sort of area that might be a friendly community — or might be a very dull place. Whatever it's like, the people living there will probably have some basic needs that will have to be met by someone. These will include: gas and electricity, shops, medical services, fire services, rubbish collection and street sweeping, public transport, housing, telephones (are these a basic need?) social services.

● Can you think of any more? Find out who runs which services — how many are run by local government, how many by nationalized industry and how many are privately run. Do you think there are some services that should be given to the community whether or not they are efficient?

● Imagine you are standing for the council in the community shown opposite. What sort of issues will concern you? How, as a councillor, do you think you will be able to help? Write a campaign speech.

● You have just moved, with your family, into the community shown opposite. Where will you go to get help with; housing problems (including getting rent and rate rebates), problems with schools, finding a job. Will you have to travel outside the area to get help?

● Imagine you are involved in running the community centre in the area shown opposite. What sort of activities and organizations do you think should be based there?

● One of the most important services is providing houses. Councils build homes for people and sometimes buy up and renovate old ones. Getting a council home can be difficult and many councils have long waiting lists. They usually award 'points' to people who have been on the list a long time or whose living conditions are very poor. Those with the most points are given homes. Find out how the 'points system' works in your area.

● From reference books, find out about the 'Parker Morris' standards for council accommodation. What problems might there be in relaxing these standards?

Ideals

What sort of place would you consider ideal?

● Carry out a survey among people you know to find out what they think makes a place good to live in. Make a graph to show which things most people think are important.

● A number of people in the past have actually tried to design perfect 'Utopian' communities. Others have simply written about them. (From reference books, find out how the word 'Utopian' came into use). Describe your own idea of a perfect community. But remember:

'This is the problem of any attempt to set up a Utopian community. How hard it is for everyone to be satisfied! (. . .) plenty of people long for a desert island or for a super city or for a cottage in the country with roses round the door, or for a mixture of town and country.'
From Utopia, by Colin Ward, Penguin Education

● Using reference books, find out about ideal communities planned by: Robert Owen, Ebenezer Howard, Clough William Ellis, William Morris, Le Corbusier.

● Imagine you have just arrived in the perfect community you described earlier. Write a script for a radio or television documentary about the place.

The perfect community? What do *you* think is important?

Community action

Case study 1: building an adventure playground

The story begins at the end of 1977 on a rather bleak housing estate in the West Country. There was no sense of community in the area, no shared facilities, not even a good bus service so that people could get away. Vandalism was a big problem — not least because there was nothing for the children on the estate to do.

One day, two women were chatting over a coffee when they hit on the idea of building an adventure playground on a piece of waste ground at one end of the estate. They approached the local authority which gave them little help: the social services department encouraged them, but no-one thought they could organize it and they were offered no money. But they did get permission to use the land for two weeks in the summer, providing they had the right insurance and cleared the site afterwards.

They began to get discouraged. Few local people seemed interested in the scheme, but in March 1978 the regional National Playing Fields Association field officer put them in touch with the local Resource Centre, an organization that, among other things, places volunteers in youth clubs. The Centre had access to printing facilities. It also had some money, and helped the women raise more and build the playground. It provided two volunteer workers.

The summer scheme was a huge success, as far as the children were concerned, though most parents and council officials avoided the place. When the scheme came to an end they had a barbecue and bonfire attended by 500 of the estate's 2 000 people.

The next step was to make the playground permanent. Local support was still hard to get, in spite of attempts to involve more people, but the two women whose idea it had been in the beginning managed to form a committee with a representative from the Resource Centre, a local policeman, a councillor and a few others.

In April 1979 they were given planning permission to go ahead with the permanent scheme, but getting the lease was difficult without the money for it, and none of the bodies that were likely to give money would do so until the women were given the lease. Eventually, with the help of some student workers drumming up local support, jumble sales and so on and a donation from the Jubilee Fund, they were able to go ahead.

Now the scheme has been running for some time and there is plenty of local support, and much more of a community feeling on the estate, thanks to two very determined women.

A place to play — frequently a rarity in city communities, but now recognised by many people as important.

Case study 2: Covent Garden

Covent Garden is an area in central London that was once the home of a large wholesale fruit and vegetable market. Now the market has closed, and the whole area has been a target for redevelopment. Over the last few years, local people have campaigned to make the area a pleasant place to live and to oppose plans for commercial development at the expense of people.

In the past, the sites of demolished buildings have been used to make community gardens. The largest of these (shown in the picture on the left) existed for over a year before it was destroyed to make way for an office block. A vigorous campaign was mounted to prevent this, but it failed. The garden was financed and worked on by local people.

The community is a very active one, with a thriving Community Association for people living and working in the area. There is a Community Centre with a bar and room for dances and other events, a youth club, a community theatre that performs in pubs all over London and a sports centre, The Jubilee Hall.

The latter, an interesting building as well as a useful one, is threatened with demolition for redevelopment, but there is a determined campaign to keep it open. This has included getting the support of local MPs, celebreties, the Victorian Society (a pressure group that works to defend Victorian buildings) and others.

● The two case studies on these pages describe two very different communities and campaigns. What sorts of events or problems do you think are most likely to bring people together?

● Think about your own area and pick out one of the problems that face people living there. The sort of things you decide on might be:

1. Plans to pull down a building that you think is attractive.
2. Lack of play space for children.
3. Dangerous roads.
4. Poor housing: bad landlords or sub-standard council housing.
5. Fumes from a local factory.

Now plan a compaign — not necessarily in real life, but as an exercise. Call a meeting. This means finding a suitable place, raising the money for room hire, writing and designing a leaflet and making sure this is delivered to local people. How would you do all this? Imagine you've got this far, and describe what you've done.

Work out what should be said at the meeting. What facts about the problem will you need to know? What sorts of reactions might you get from the people whose job it is to deal with the problem? Again, describe your 'experiences'.

Look into ways of giving your campaign publicity — does the local paper take this sort of thing up? Can local radio help?

Plan a newsletter, designing several issues to show how your campaign progresses.

Outsiders: labels, problems and people

The statistics below have been chosen almost at random. Do you think they tell you very much?

One family in 10 has only one parent.
In 1975, 4 000 women and 13 000 men were admitted into hospital as alcoholics. Alcoholism is a faster-growing problem among women than among men.
In 1976, there were 4 532 000 men over 60 and 6 504 000 women over 60; 60 000 children were taken into care; there were 1 881 registered drug addicts and only 23.7 per cent of all under-fives had any education.

Many different kinds of people have problems that mean that they need some sort of support from others. We tend to talk of them collectively, but once they are seen as numbers instead of people, they become rather easier for the rest of us to forget. All those statistics are people, each one different from the next.

But when people are talking about 'problems' rather than people they may generalize and make statements that are quite unlikely to be applicable to many of the people concerned.

What's it like to be a statistic?

'What do these old people think? What gets me is the feeling that these old people have just been planted here (in an old people's hospital) and that's it. Relatives are happy. The problem has been solved. But the men are just shrivelling up. No one is trying to keep their minds going. Their bodies are kept clean, but this ain't home is it?'
A worker in a geriatric hospital

● Now imagine you are a relative of one of the people in the hospital and explain why you wanted him put there.

Those who feel that it's best to be at home, as well as those who think it will save the country money, often talk about 'community care' as an alternative to specialist hostels and hospitals for the old, handicapped, mentally handicapped or disturbed and so on.

But, as every person is different, so their needs are different. 'Community care' is a good idea if it suits the person concerned and if it really means *care* — if there are friendly neighbours, good social services, sympathetic families, enough money, comfortable housing and so on.

But if no one is prepared to do much, it might mean nothing more than loneliness and discomfort.

● Read the case study about Miss G and look at the photographs opposite. Imagine that one of these people has kept a diary and write the entries for a few days, explaining what has happened and how the person writing felt about it.
● You are the mother of a handicapped child. Describe how this has affected your day-to-day life and why you do or do not want to send your child away from home.
● Find out some of the reasons why a young person or child might be put into 'care' or a foster home.
● Is there a home for mentally handicapped people, or for elderly people in your area? Are these places thought of as a part of the community, or do the people that live in them lead quite separate lives?

A group of clergymen and their wives had regular meetings with their local MP to discuss social problems in the constituency. One of the wives said she thought that there ought to be a refuge in the area for battered women. One of the clergyman turned to her husband and said: 'What have you been doing to her?'
Do you think he would have asked the question if he had known a woman whose husband had injured her? How do you think he might have reacted if he had met such a person? Or if he had been one himself?

Opposite page, top: luncheon clubs can provide welcome company as well as a tasty meal — without too much expense. Bread and tea (below) isn't really enough. Above (this page): help and comfort from a district nurse.

Case study for a social worker

Miss G was an elderly lady who used to live in a flat in her landlord's house. The landlord — who wanted her out — said she was 'smelling him out of house and home', that she was more or less immobile and would not admit that she had problems.

A social worker met the landlord and Miss G. Miss G said little, but did not seem to be in anything like as bad a way as the landlord had suggested. She did, though, refuse any help — home help, health visitor, even a stick to help her walk, though she had arthritis. But she did accept a 'meals on wheels' service.

Next, a neighbour called the social worker in. She had been helping Miss G with cleaning and shopping for some years, and now all help was being refused. When the social worker visited, Miss G said the neighbour was bossy, she didn't need her help and that a local shop keeper was delivering her groceries. Her room was very cold. Miss G agreed to let the social social worker sort out one problem — that Miss G's doctor had retired some years earlier and she needed to find a new one.

A local GP the landlord knew socially paid a visit. A district nurse was to come and help her bath and a home help was organized.

But then the GP then 'referred this case to a "proper officer" for investigation of a Section 47 removal.' This meant that he wanted permission to have her taken away from home in spite of her wishes.

She was admitted to an old people's hostel, it was said she was suffering from an illness. It was true she had ulcers on her legs but this needn't have meant taking her away from home. In any case, she was soon better and wanted to return to her flat. But by this time the landlord had re-let it and she had to stay in the hostel. She died of 'flu only a few weeks later.

● Act out the meeting between the landlord, the social worker and Miss G. Remember that Miss G is elderly and confused, but not really ill or difficult, and that the landlord is probably more interested in letting the flat she lives in than in Miss G's welfare.

● What would you think if you heard anyone saying these things about you, or one of your friends?
'Of course, her parents have split up, so she's bound to be troublesome. They always are.'
'I can't think why he doesn't just pull himself together and sort himself out.'
'Old people get miserable because they don't have enough to do. All they have to do is keep busy.'
'It's really much better to put people like that away in a home.'
'They ought to help themselves instead of expecting us to do it for them.'
'What's the point in keeping them alive?'

Outsiders: strangers in a strange land

'Kenneth Warren, isolated on a tea garden in upper Assam some years before the Great War, always made a point of dressing for dinner: "If you lost your self-respect you were not looked upon in a respectful and proper manner." '

'The early morning often saw (. . .) sporting activities (. . .) some transplanted direct from the English sporting scene. "In Lahore and Peshawar we had a hunt. We didn't hunt foxes, but jackals. We had fox-hounds imported from England, and we had marvellous days, just as good as a hunt in England except that there weren't so many hedges to jump." '

'The memsahib of the twenties and thirties did her best to keep up with her English counterpart. Fashions were followed as far as the climate allowed. The inappropriate costumes of the previous decade — "Lots of underclothes and heavy skirts down to the ankles" — were abandoned for practical informality. "I look back," recalls Mrs Lee of the Edwardian era, "and marvel how we survived." '
From Plain Tales from the Raj, edited by Charles Allen, BBC

The quotations above are taken from a book about the British in India in the early part of this century, when it was still part of a large and prosperous empire.

The people speaking are fairly privileged. They had plenty of money and servants and could afford to live in a style few Indians (or working class people in Britain) could afford. They went to India as rulers.

But, in a sense, they were immigrants. They had left their own homes and settled in a new country — the difference between those immigrants and most others is that they arrived as a ruling class.

Like other immigrants, they tried to keep to their own customs (those of upper class people at home, though perhaps a little exaggerated or rather behind the times). They mixed only with one another — hardly ever meeting Indians socially.

People who share a culture, values or attitudes naturally prefer to live together. When immigrants from countries that had once been the Empire came to Britain to work, they also sought the company of other people with the same background.

Top: the British in India held on firmly to their own customs and styles of dress — however inappropriate. Left, a young Sikh in London. Notice the Punjabi writing.

Europe's gipsies, or Rom, came from India in the 900s. Since then, they have suffered frequent persecution and harrassment. They are travellers, preferring a wandering life, maintaining their own language and traditions. Unable to tolerate this, many states have tried to make them settle down — either directly by making them live in certain places, or indirectly by making it hard for them to find places to camp.
● From reference books, find out as much as you can about gipsy communities. Do you know if there is any provision for them in your own area? What do local people think of gipsies? Are they prejudiced against them?

Media coverage

'The media in this country is very powerful. It is not like in our country where many people cannot read and write. The media here has played a very bad role so far as race relations is concerned. The media should have been working to restore confidence in the minority. Instead, the media has created uncertainty in our community.'
Ajit Singh Rai, from People talking: New Commonwealth immigrants by Nance Lui Fyson and Sally Greenhill, Macmillan Education

● Collect a variety of newspapers and study their coverage of immigrants, immigration and race. Look for statements from politicians about numbers of immigrants. How often are black people in the news in a positive way – as successful or interesting people? Do you agree with Ajit Singh Rai?

More labels

Immigrants and racial minorities suffer from the same sort of labelling as the old and handicapped people described on the previous page. Here is a description of some people at a meeting where race is being discussed:
'. . . (they) are not bad people. They have learned from television and newspapers to talk about ''coloured'' people and to lump together the most varied human beings as ''coloured'' and so all alike, regardless of different culture, language
(. . .) They are unaware how potty it is to think that because one man from Pakistan was rude to someone last month, all Jamaicans, Barbadians, Trinidadians, Ghanaians, Arabs and Indians are likely to be rude next Tuesday.'
From A Portrait of English Racism by Ann Dummett, Pelican

● Look again at your collection of newspapers and see if you can find any evidence of this kind of 'labelling' prejudice. How often is the word 'immigrant' used to mean 'black'? (This is really a misuse of the word).

'Integration'

'One thing that worries her is the Pakistanis; they will wear national dress when they come over here, and she thinks that if these people are going to come over here they ought to adapt to our ways (. . .) Would she wear a tunic and shalwars if she went to live in West Pakistan? No, she wouldn't.'
From A Portrait of English Racism

● Do you think that people with a different background and culture ought to 'integrate' into the culture they are living in by dropping all their traditions, or do you think that a multicultural society is a good thing? Why? What do you think the people in India, quoted opposite, would have thought about 'integrating' into Indian culture?

● You've been offered a job in a foreign country. The place is a long way from your home, and very different. You will not be very important when you get there, but you have the chance of earning more money than you would at home. You decide to take the job. When you arrive you find that few people speak your language, and those that do have learned English in America and don't always understand what you say.

You feel very lonely. Only one thing helps. There are a few other British people living in the country. You don't know any of them personally, but you think you will get some help from them, particularly in finding somewhere to live.

Write a series of letters home, describing how you arrived, how you felt at the time, what you did next, how you found somewhere to live, what your job is like and what the other people in the country are like. How do you make yourself feel at home? What do you miss most?

Healthy living

'At the back of the house a (. . .) dairyman kept in large sheds about 40 milk cows. (. . .) The cows were turned out every day into a large yard which was only divided from our premises by a low wall. The smell was at times intolerable, and the flies in summer were a perfect plague. Sanitation was never considered. The water butt was placed outside the closet, which had no flush and smelt abominably. The ashes and house refuse were put in one corner of the yard only a few yards from the water butt. This applied to all the other houses in the neighbourhood. As a result of the bad sanitation epidemics of various kinds of fevers and of smallpox broke out. On one occasion cholera was so bad that many hundreds died.'
Mrs Layton, from Life as We Have Known it by Co-operative Working Women, edited by Margaret Llewellyn Davies, Virago. Time: the 1860s

Disease is rife where there is poor sanitation, poor food and overcrowded living conditions. The statistics below show how all these factors, along with limited medical knowledge, worked together in the past to produce high death rates among children and low average ages for deaths. The almost sudden drop in infant mortality shown in the diagram was the result of better housing, better education, diet and smaller families as much as improvements in medicine. The appalling squalor of a Victorian slum is rarely (though by no means never) found in Britain today, but this is not the case in other parts of the world where poverty, disease and early death go hand in hand.

Average age at death, 1840

	Gentry, etc.	Tradesmen	Labourers
Liverpool:	35	22	15
Wiltshire:	50	48	33

Infant mortality per thousand live births (from 0–1 year)

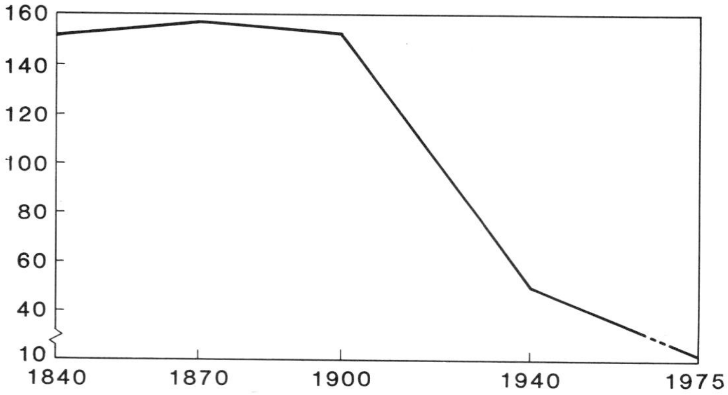

In the past, poverty and ignorance brought early death.

The National Health Service

● **The health service operates in a variety of ways (see the *Topic Book*). Look up the history of the National Health Service to find out when, how it was founded, and how it is run today. Do you think there is still a need for a free medical service for everyone?**

● Look up in reference books and find out about the lives and work of Dr John Snow, Edward Jenner, Lord Shaftesbury and George Peabody.

● Find out about the average ages of deaths and infant mortality in India. How do these compare with Britain today? Why do you think they are different?

Some parts of the country have particular problems with diseases related to local industries, such as in coal mining, pottery manufacture and among people who have worked with asbestos.

Breathing in polluted air, lead fumes and car exhausts can also be damaging to health, particularly among young children.

● Do you think your area is a healthy one? Give your reasons. What could be done to improve matters?

Case study 1: Norton Medical Centre

Norton Medical centre in Stockton-on-Tees began many years ago as an ordinary general practice. Today it is a community-based medical centre offering a variety of services to 1700 of the people living within a three-mile radius.

The area covered is socially mixed, with the proportions of each class being about the same as the national average. There is one area of poor housing where the risks to health are high, especially among mothers-to-be and young babies.

Norton, which is not a local authority health centre, has five doctors as well as nurses, midwives, a psychiatric nurse, clerical staff, the voluntary help of two marriage guidance councillors and liaison with a local authority social worker and the local vicar.

Staff at the centre have an especially close relationship with the community. Up to a point, they will seek out patients rather than simply waiting for them to turn up. This can mean, for example, that if someone is bitten by a dog and forgets their second anti-tetanus injection, they'll get a note reminding them to come into the surgery. Mothers and mothers-to-be have the facilities of a well-woman clinic and a well-baby clinic. Because women know the centre and find it easy to reach with less waiting around than in a hospital, attendance is good and the result is that the perinatal mortality rate (the deaths of babies from the 28th week of the mother's pregnancy to the first week after birth) is only 10 in 1 000 rather than the national average of 17 in 1 000. Ninety per cent of babies are immunized, which is much higher than the national average.

Case study 2: Community doctor

The Guy's Health District in South London is making an attempt to solve some of the health problems in the local community by trying to spot them early. There is a Child Health Community Service that employs 10 doctors. These work in school clinics and run nursery school medicals. There is an infant welfare service (for children from 0 to six months) and checks are made on health and diet. If necessary they are referred to a hospital for specialist treatment. If a parent and child do not turn up for an appointment, parents are reminded three times to bring the child to the service's Centre.

The aim is to catch health problems early, and the result has been fewer emergency admissions to hospital. Like the staff at the Norton Medical Centre, the doctors working for this service are interested in seeking out the people who have problems, rather than waiting for them to turn up. In addition to that, the doctors get to know their patients better.

- From the information given above and your own researches say what a community doctor or health centre can do that an ordinary GP cannot? Can you think of any disadvantages in community medicine?
- Plan a radio programme about health services in your area. What would the following people have to say about their work: a midwife, a district nurse, a doctor, and a health visitor? What would a working woman, reluctant to spare the time for an ante-natal clinic say? Or an old man, wheelchair-bound?
- Design a poster to advertise some of the facilities at a local health centre.

The team at the Norton Medical centre. The staff work democratically — day-to-day decisions about care are made by the appropriate people (nurses, social workers and so on). In many practices, by contrast, it is common for most decisions to be made by doctors and a team's work to be less evenly divided.

Policy for the centre is decided by a house committee made up of representatives from all the staff. The team keep in close touch with the community they serve and are given help in this by the local vicar and a local authority social worker.

Destruction rules — OK?

Vandalism is . . .

Mindless destruction. . . the result of boredom. . . just a bit of fun. . . just kids. . . a protest against a de-humanizing society. . .

How would you define vandalism? The usual definition is that it is the destruction of property for no reason. Most of what is usually accepted as vandalism is committed by young people — often children.

It has been said that vandalism is not only a matter of *what* is done but also of who does it. Few people see themselves as vandals. A young couple carving their names into the bark of a tree are defacing it — but they'll probably think of themselves as being old-fashioned and rather romantic. Are students carrying out 'rag' stunts vandals, or just high spirited? Would you call a destructive five-year-old a vandal?

Fighting vandalism

There are two main ways in which communities try to put a stop to vandalism. One is by being very tough with vandals, putting extra police in an area or by dealing out heavy fines and other punishments. Another way is by community action, solving the problems of boredom and anger that often lie behind vandalism.

You can read about one community based campaign against vandalism on page 29 of the *Topic Book*. Opposite is a description of how a community in Scotland tackled the problem of being in a run-down area where petty crime and vandalism were rife.

Something to do

- Some people feel that developers and builders who destroy old buildings and change parts of towns are vandals as much as teenagers who wreck a telephone box. Give some examples of this 'official' vandalism.
- Vandalism can be dangerous. Can you think of examples of how this might be so?
- Find out if anyone in your class has ever vandalized anything. Why did they do it?
- Write an article as if for a local paper about vandalism in your area. You could include comments from local people, with ideas about how to solve the problem.
- Write a letter, as if to the same paper, about developers,plans to pull down an old building you think is a valuable part of the environment.

Nooligan

I'm a nooligan
dont give a toss
in our class
I'm the boss
(well, one of them)

I'm a nooligan
got a nard 'ead
step out of line
and youre dead
(well, bleedin)

I'm a nooligan
I spray me name
all over town
footballs me game
(well, watchin)

I'm a nooligan
violence is fun
gonna be a nassassin
or a nired gun
(well, a soldier)

Roger McGough

Case study: Gibshill

Gibshill is a housing estate near Greenock. In the early 1970s it was a sad place, with high unemployment, neglected housing and a serious vandalism problem. In the early 1970s, local people formed a Tenants' Association. One of its jobs was to make local opinion clear to the council, which had decided to give the area a facelift.

One member of the Tenants' Association took particular interest in the problems of the young people of the area. He started a disco for 10-12 year olds. Then the older teenagers asked him if something could be done for them — they wanted a place to meet, and they wanted the police to leave them alone. The Tenants' Association spoke to local police leaders and managed to have the number of 'panda' patrols cut down in favour of beat policemen who knew local people better. A club for the older teenagers was started in a derelict contractors hut (repaired and repainted by the users). Once open, the club was run by local tenants and a committee of the young people. In 1976, a special youth hall built by the local authority was opened.

The council's plans for the area were discussed fully by local people, and helpful suggestions made. For example, the council planned that a pub should be built in one new development. Local people decided that this should not be owned by a brewery with an interest in selling a lot of drink, but should be a club controlled by the tenants.

One result of the community action was that in less than four years the number of crimes committed by young people was halved and the whole area had aquired a new reputation.
Source: People Power by Tony Gibson, Pelican. From chapter 4: Gibshill Puts Down Crime.

A local campaign

● Survey the area around your home or school, making a record of all the vandalism you see. If possible, take photographs. With the knowledge of the area you have gained from earlier work, suggest some reasons for the vandalism (or, if there is very little, suggest reasons for this instead).

● Design a poster and badges for an anti-vandalism campaign.

'It looks good to see your name', a young vandal once told a reporter. If so, this bridge must look good to a lot of people. But does it? Vandalism in this form is unsightly, but not actually dangerous. Damage to the railway track itself might be a different story, especially if there was an accident. Other common forms of vandalism include damage to communal property, such as telephone boxes.

Graffitti with a message. Whoever wrote this was making a conscious protest about a serious problem in today's cities — homelessness. Witty, eye-catching or political slogans are a kind of vandalism that many people feel is almost an art form.

Alternatives

Case study 1: The People's Commune

The sorts of communities that exist in Britain have grown up over the years and are part of a system: of being an industrial country, of expecting people to live in cities, near the industry, of land being privately owned, of people living in family groups and so on.

In China, a new kind of community has been set up — the People's Commune. Before China's revolution, which ended in 1949, land was owned mainly by landlords and richer peasants. Other country people were often very poor. After the revolution, the state took over the land and set up collective farms. Later, these were grouped together to form People's Communes. As well as being groups of farms these were administrative units, supplying services such as health care and schools.

There are about 5 000 households in a commune. Families are organized into production teams, along with their neighbours. The teams in turn work in production brigades, whose responsibility it is to plan production targets, to organize leisure and cultural activities and to administer commune policy and collective enterprises such as workshops, stores and veterinary services.

Production brigades form the commune, which is run by a committee of representatives of the people living there. The commune's contact with the administration of the country is

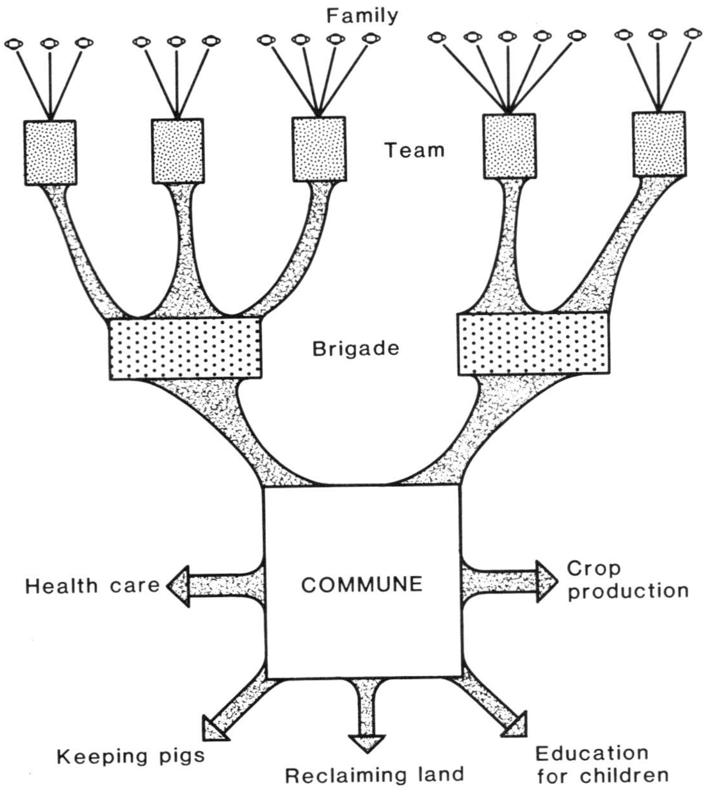

The structure of a People's Commune

Threshing corn on a commune. The commune, made up of brigades (which are in turn made up of teams) is responsible for food production and is a social unit — providing schooling, medical services and so on for its members.

The sorts of things a commune can be responsible for are illustrated in the diagram above.

through this Revolutionary committee.

Communes are designed so that the people living in them can take part in the decisions that affect them. It is also a way of sharing out land. It is a community designed to fit in with a certain kind of political system, and to overcome specific problems — mainly how to share out land and still operate efficient farming methods.

● Read about China before and after the revolution. How is today's system of land distribution different from that before the revolution?

● Write about a farming community in which several people are working together. Most want to work as a team — one would prefer to work alone and does not want to help the others. Write a story about that person, and what she or he had to say to the other people in the community.

Case study 2: Patchwork

The Patchwork communities were started about nine years ago in London. They were designed to provide an alternative life-style for people who did not want to live in nuclear family groups and to provide something other than institutional life for those who had had problems with, for example, drugs or who had a background of prison, or similar problems. 'We wanted to get away from the idea of hostels for ex-this and ex-that' said one founder member.

The communities are made up of a variety of people of different backgrounds and ages, ranging from young children to people in their 70s. Most are in 'short life' housing — property which has been bought by local authorities and is awaiting conversion and rehabilitation.

Community members are not cut off from the outside world. Many work outside the community and have friends who do not live there.

One of the first long term communities to be formed by Patchwork is in west London. It consists of three large houses joined together, with large kitchens, plenty of bathrooms and a bedroom for each single person or couple. Household tasks, though not divided on a rota basis are shared out — people do them whenever they think it's necessary and this seems to work most of the time.

In some instances, individuals have made themselves responsible for a particular aspect of community life. One man, for example, has taken over the houses, finances. Everyone gives 60 per cent of his or her income to the house to pay for rent and food and so on. This means things can be bought in bulk, making them cheaper.

Collective living like this is a good system for one-parent families. Children can be brought up together and the parents can share the work of looking after them, giving them some time to themselves.

There are no formal rules, though community members do feel a commitment to the people they live with. One member, who had spent a year doing a full-time college course, and had depended on the community to help her look after her son in that time, admits to feeling a conflict of commitments: 'I felt bad being out all day'.

Problems are usually sorted out as they turn up but there is a monthly meeting to discuss money.

● You are planning to form a community of about 10 people. Who would you choose? Would they all be the same age? Would they all have the same interests? Would you have any rules — and if so, what would they be?

● The cartoon shows a community that has a few problems. The people living in it have a weekly meeting. Act out the meeting. What do you think each person will say about the job that he or she has not done? What suggestions will be made about improving things?

● Look at the chapter on organized communities in the *Topic Book.* Can you suggest some reasons why the community the cartoon shows might not be working?

● Find out all you can about life in a convent or a monastery. What sorts of rules do people in religious communities have to keep? Why do you think they choose to keep these rules rather than live a 'freer' life outside? How do religious communities try to make sure that no one joins unless he or she is really certain it's the right decision?

The future

Times change. The jobs people have, the things they want and the lifestyles they expect all change too. Traditional customs and ideas disappear when new industries and new circumstances appear and force change on people.

The kinds of communities we live in today are different from those in which our ancestors lived. They are probably very different from those our descendants will live in.

Change, of course, needn't always be for the best, or for that matter, for the worst.

These are just some of the possible changes that might be seen in the next hundred or so years:

1. Energy sources (coal, oil, gas and nuclear fuel) may begin to disappear and become very expensive. Travel becomes impossible, life becomes dismal and uncomfortable. Industry declines, millions are out of work and in great poverty.
2. New energy sources are found. There is work, wealth and resources for everyone, and plenty of leisure.
3. Energy sources are found, but new technological developments mean that though there is wealth for some, most people are out of work and poor.
4. There is a world war. Millions of people are wiped out. Only a few remain to rebuild society.

● Work out what community life might be like in these or any other circumstances you can imagine. What sorts or rules might people need in order to live peacefully? What sorts of aims and ideals might they have?

Remains from today

The picture below shows a suggestion how a community might solve a problem of a shortage of food. It would mean working together. It would also mean making the best of things that are there already — in this case, the space taken up by individual gardens at the back of a terrace of houses. No new kind of community life is likely to grow up without anything left over from the old. Whatever happens in the future, the houses, roads, railways and so on we have today or their remains are likely to stay with us. When you describe your community of the future, try to take into account the left-overs from today's communities. These left-overs will be more than material things — they will include the values, attitudes, the ideas of right and wrong we have today.

A possible solution to a food problem — but it would need more co-operation among neighbours than we are used to now.